MATH MAZES
Times Tables

by Angelika Scudamore

ARCTURUS

W9-BKF-683

ARCTURUS

This edition published in 2019 by Arcturus Publishing Limited
26/27 Bickels Yard, 151–153 Bermondsey Street,
London SE1 3HA

Copyright © Arcturus Holdings Limited

All rights reserved. No part of this publication may be reproduced,
stored in a retrieval system, or transmitted, in any form or by any means,
electronic, mechanical, photocopying, recording or otherwise, without
prior written permission in accordance with the provisions of the
Copyright Act 1956 (as amended). Any person or persons who do any
unauthorised act in relation to this publication may be liable to criminal
prosecution and civil claims for damages.

Edited by Sebastian Rydberg
Written by William Potter
Illustrated by Angelika Scudamore
Designed by Trudi Webb

ISBN: 978-1-78950-023-3
CH006622NT
Supplier 29, Date 0319, Print run 7813

Printed in China

How to Use This Book

Welcome to the "funtastic" world of times tables mazes! This book is full of exciting mazes to help you learn the basics of multiplication and division.

Locate the start of each maze, and read the instructions to help you solve it.

Solve each calculation, and then choose the correct path to reach the end.

Divide by 8
Solve the problems and follow the route with the correct answers to lead the shoppers to the check out.

start

96÷8

54

48÷8

7   32÷8

5   5   72÷8

6   4   8

64÷8   6

12   11   16÷8   40÷8   9

11   8   1   4   88÷8

80÷8   2   3

10   12   24÷8   11   12

96÷8   0   PAY HERE

Finish

38   39

Top Tip
Remember that division is the opposite of multiplication.

Some topics come with a Top Tip to help you on the way.

If you are stuck you can always check the answers on pages 89-96.

Doubles

Guide the fairy back to her toadstool home. Follow the problems that are doubles. Watch out for the gnomes!

Start

2+4

3+3

3+4

8+8

6+6

4+4

5+5

9+8

Top Tip

A double is where two numbers the same are added together.
Double 3 = 3 + 3

4

Multiples of 2

Lead the astronaut through the stardust back to the rocket. Follow the numbers that are multiples of 2.

start

7

9

16

2

8

12

15

23

6

Top Tip

Multiples of 2 are numbers in the two times table. Multiples of 2 can be divided by 2.

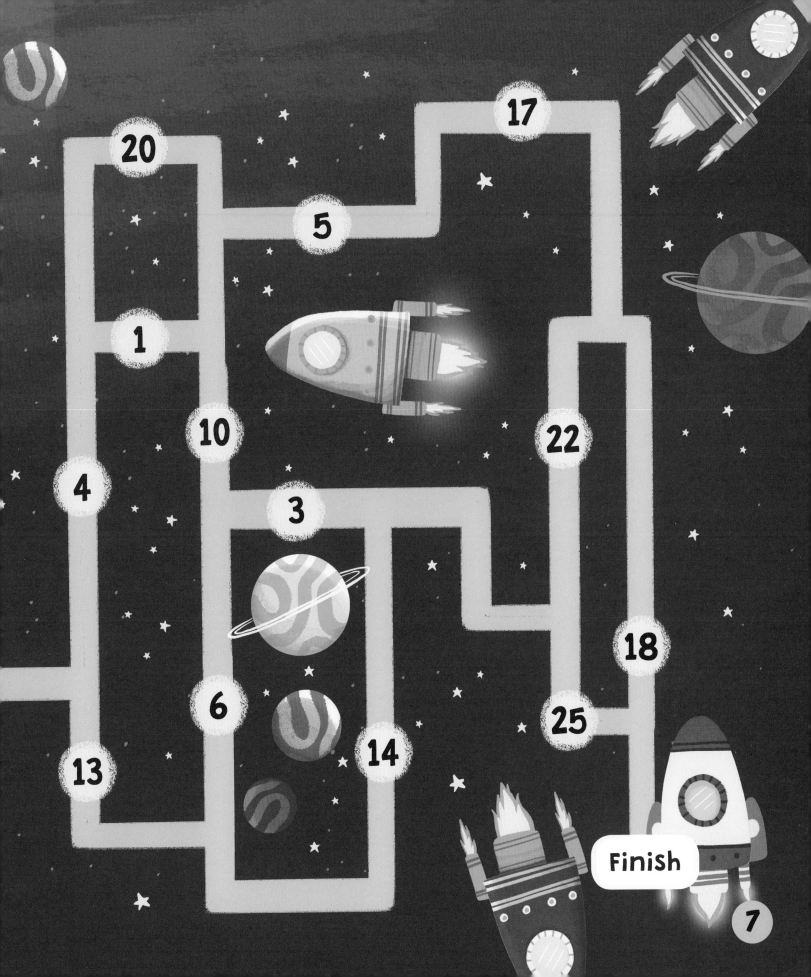

Multiples by 2

Help the girl to find her friend at the skate park.
Work out the calculations and follow
the correct answers.

24

2×12

22

14   10

2×6

12

2×5

Start

14

2×4

12

8

8

Top Tip

2 x 4 = 2 + 2 + 2 + 2

Finish

9

Divide by 2

Can you guide the boy across the city in time to watch the movie? Work out the calculations and follow the correct answers.

5

12

10÷2

10

2

12÷2

8

4÷2

6

4÷2

Start

4

2

11

22÷2

12

14

6

24÷2

16÷2

8

6

10

Top Tip
Dividing by 2 is the same as halving the number.

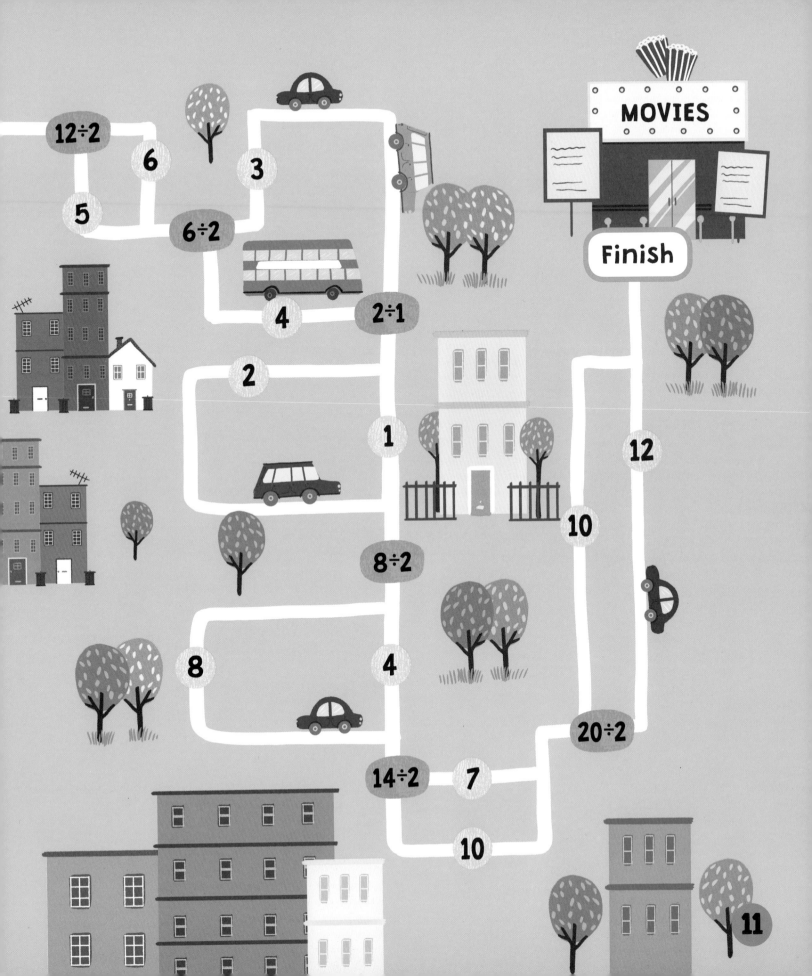

Multiples of 10

Help the knight to find his horse. Follow all of the numbers that are multiples of 10.

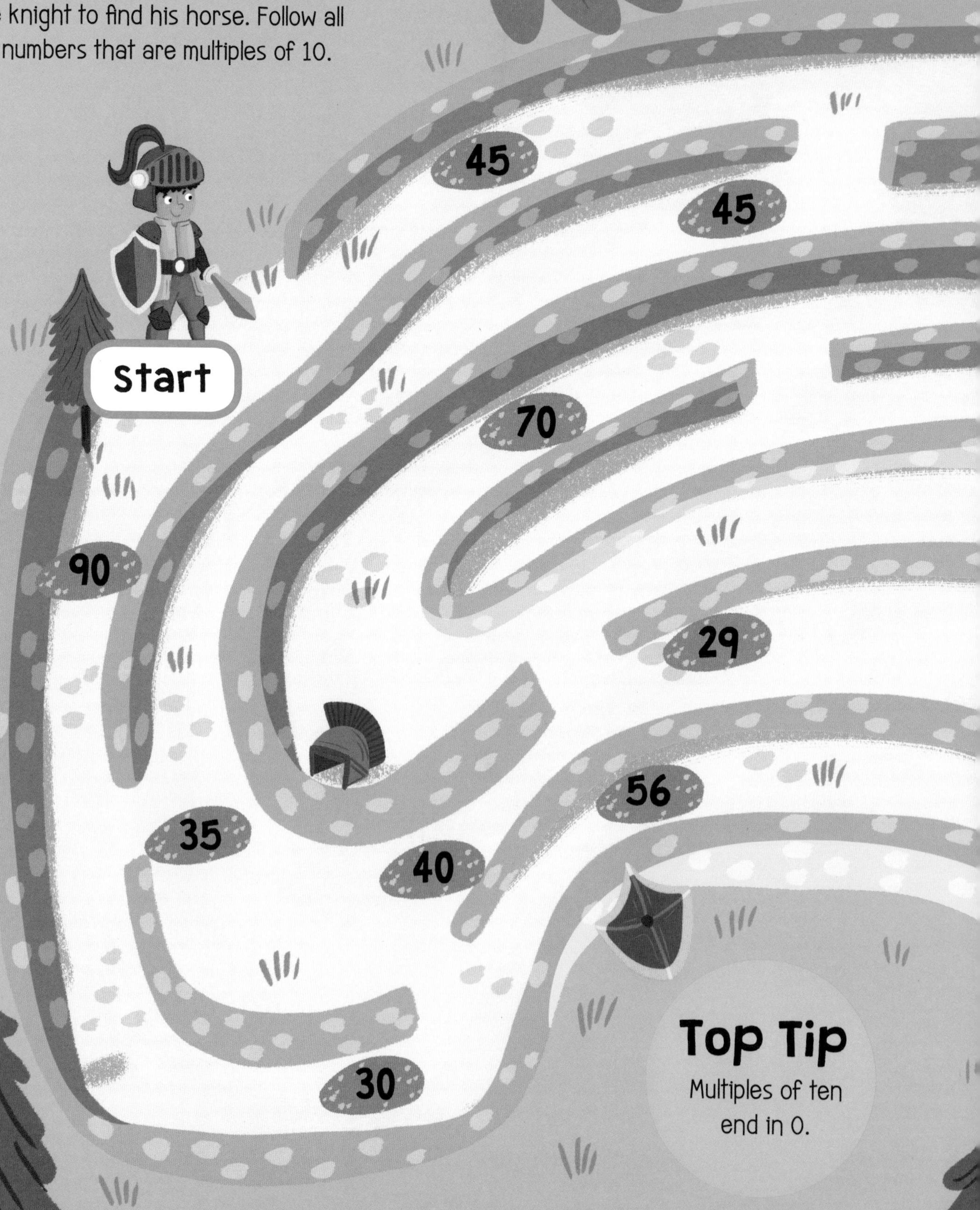

Start

45

45

70

90

29

35

56

40

30

Top Tip

Multiples of ten end in 0.

75

32

80

85

81

10

65

50

20

110

120

Finish

13

Multiples of 10

The boy is eager to start skiing.
Can you guide him to the ski lift?
Work out the calculations.

44

100

10×4

Start

40

10

10×10

10×9

50

19

90

55

10×5

Top Tip
Multiples of ten
end in 0.

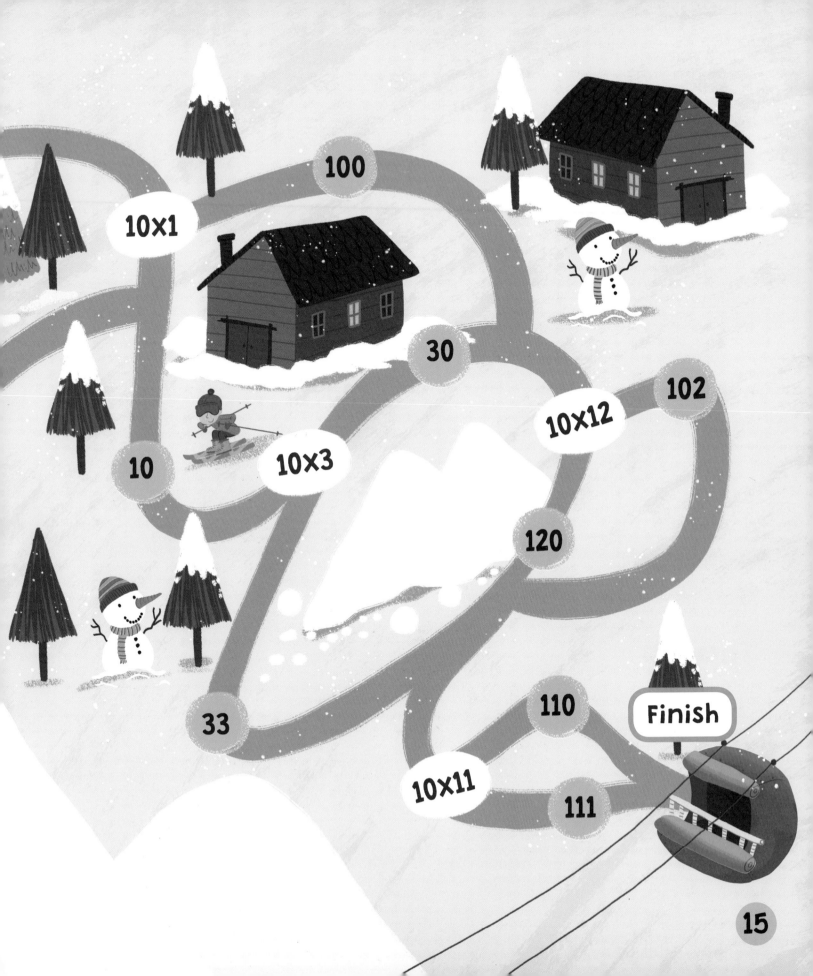

100

10×1

30

102

10×12

10×3

10

120

33

110

Finish

10×11

111

15

Divide by 10

The elephant wants a drink. Can you lead him to the water?
Solve the problems and follow the correct answers to reach the waterfall.

Start

$40 \div 10$

10

5

$50 \div 10$

$70 \div 10$

500

70

4

20

120 ÷ 10

Top Tip
Remember division is the opposite of multiplication:
$7 \times 10 = 70$
$70 \div 10 = 7$

12

3

$30 \div 10$

6

16

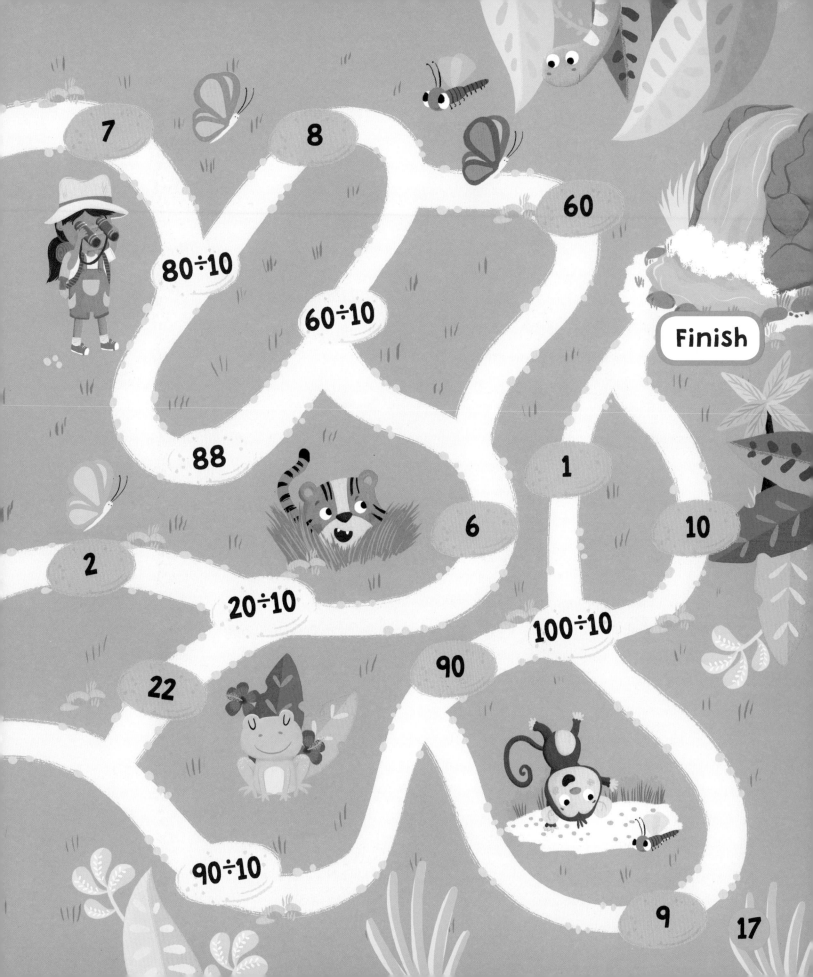

7

8

60

80÷10

60÷10

Finish

88

1

10

6

2

20÷10

100÷10

22

90

90÷10

9

17

Multiples of 5

Lead the camel across the desert.
Follow the numbers that are multiples of 5.

58

17

65

20

Start

30

45

23

14

Top Tip

Multiples of 5 end in 0 or 5.

18

Multiples of 5

Guide the children out of the maze. Solve the calculations and follow the route with the correct answers.

Start

5X1

20

5X4

5

55

25

5X5

35

25

30

5X7

Top Tip

Try counting in 5s.

20

Divide by 5

Can you guide the little fish away from the shark before it's too late? Solve the calculations and follow the trail with the correct answers.

start

25÷5

8

45÷5

11

55÷5

10

7

40÷5

20

5

1

0

35÷5

7

5÷5

8

22

Top Tip
Use your multiplication facts to help you.

Mixed multiples 2, 5, and 10

Can you show the girl to the music room in time for her music lesson? Solve the multiplication problems and follow the correct answers.

Start

2x10

15

50

50

10x5

20

4

2x5

10

2x2

8

7

24

Mixed division 2, 5, and 10

By solving the calculations and following the correct answers, lead the children to the ice cream van on the beach.

40

45÷5

8

20÷5

5

80÷10

4

2

5

11

4

55÷5

25÷5

Start

Top Tip
Make sure you share by the correct amount.

Multiples of 4

Follow the numbers that are multiples of 4 and guide the children to the sandpit to play.

start

16

44

12

26

36

8

4

40

22

24

28

Top Tip

All the answers in the 4 times table are even numbers.

Multiples of 4

Can you navigate around the map to find the elephant enclosure at the zoo? Solve the multiplication problems and follow the route with the correct answers.

31

26

4x8

32

4x7

28

4x12

Start

36

4x9

34

Top Tip

Multiplying by 4 is the same as doubling and doubling again:
(7 + 7) + (7 + 7) = 28

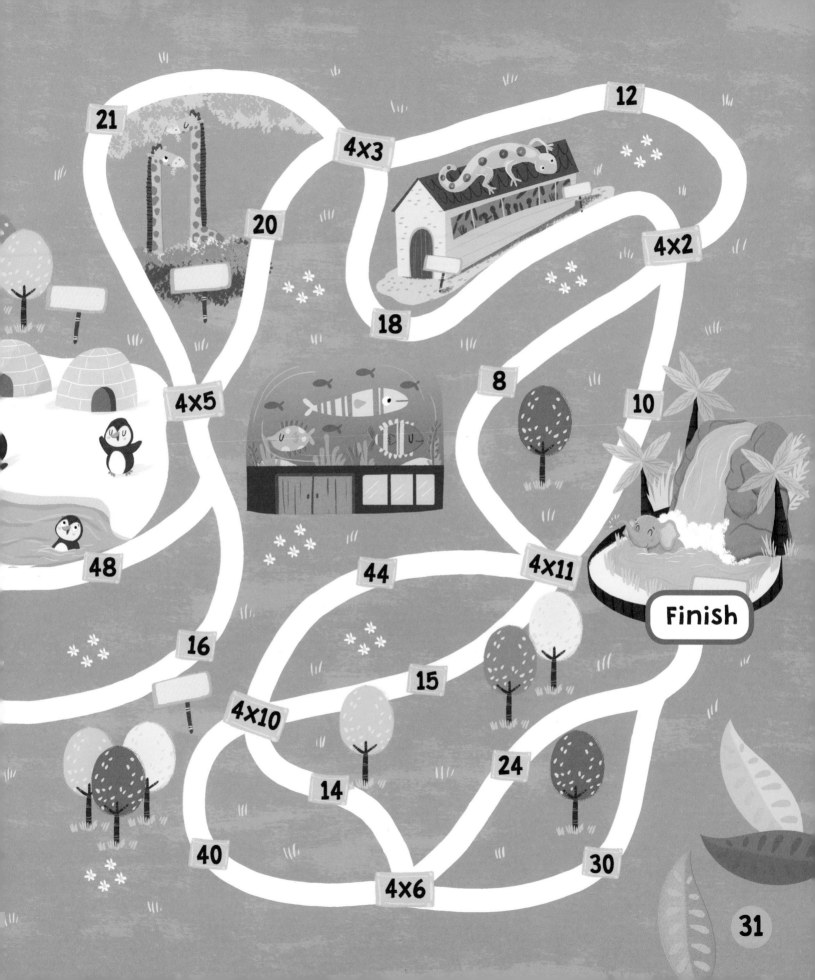

21

4×3

12

20

4×2

18

4×5

8

10

48

44

4×11

Finish

16

15

4×10

24

14

40

30

4×6

31

Divide by 4

Can you guide the train through the countryside to the station? Solve the problems and follow the path with the correct answers.

Start

$36÷4$

$32÷4$

8

$48÷4$

8

7

8

7

$28÷4$

9

Top Tip

Use your knowledge of the 4 times table to help you:
$32 ÷ 4 = 8$
$8 × 4 = 32$

5

12

20÷4

11

4

16÷4

3

8÷4

4

11

40÷4

0

24÷4

7

6

4

48

44÷4

2

10

Finish

33

Multiples of 8

Follow the numbers that are multiples of 8 and guide the ants across the garden and back to their nest.

Start

8

20

48

64

56

18

10

16

Top Tip

If you can't remember your 8 times table, double the answers in the 4 times table.

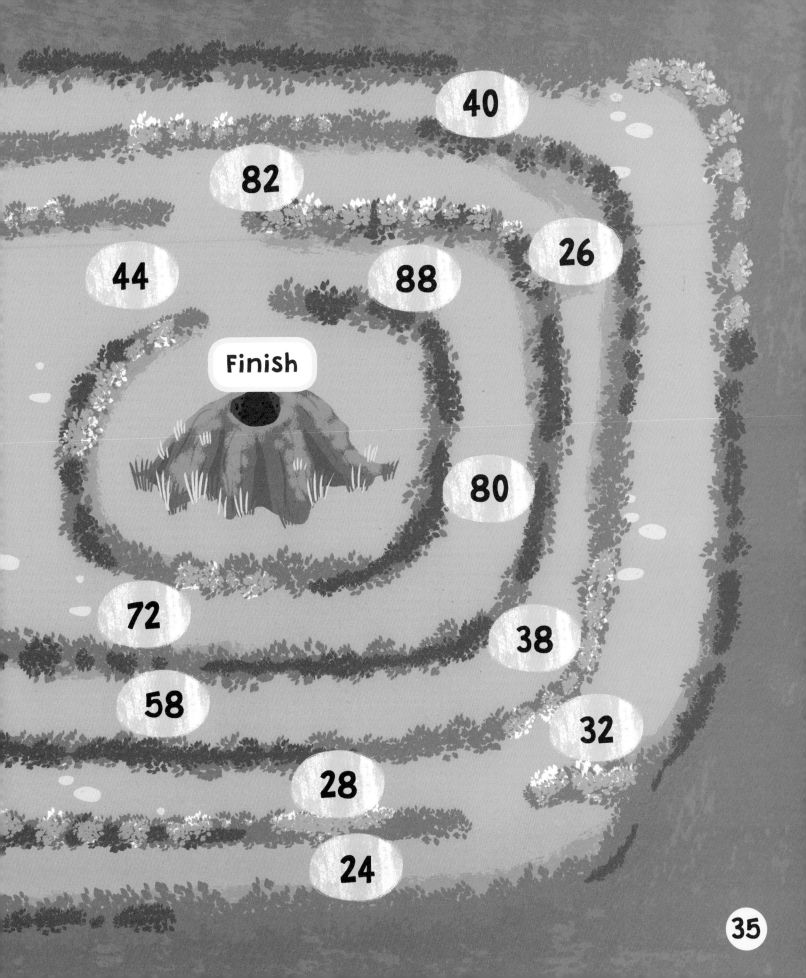

Multiples of 8

Answer the calculations and follow the trail with the correct answers to help the dinosaur find her eggs before the volcano erupts!

64

8X6

8X8

68

10

16

8X2

35

80

40

Start

8X5

8X4

18

30

32

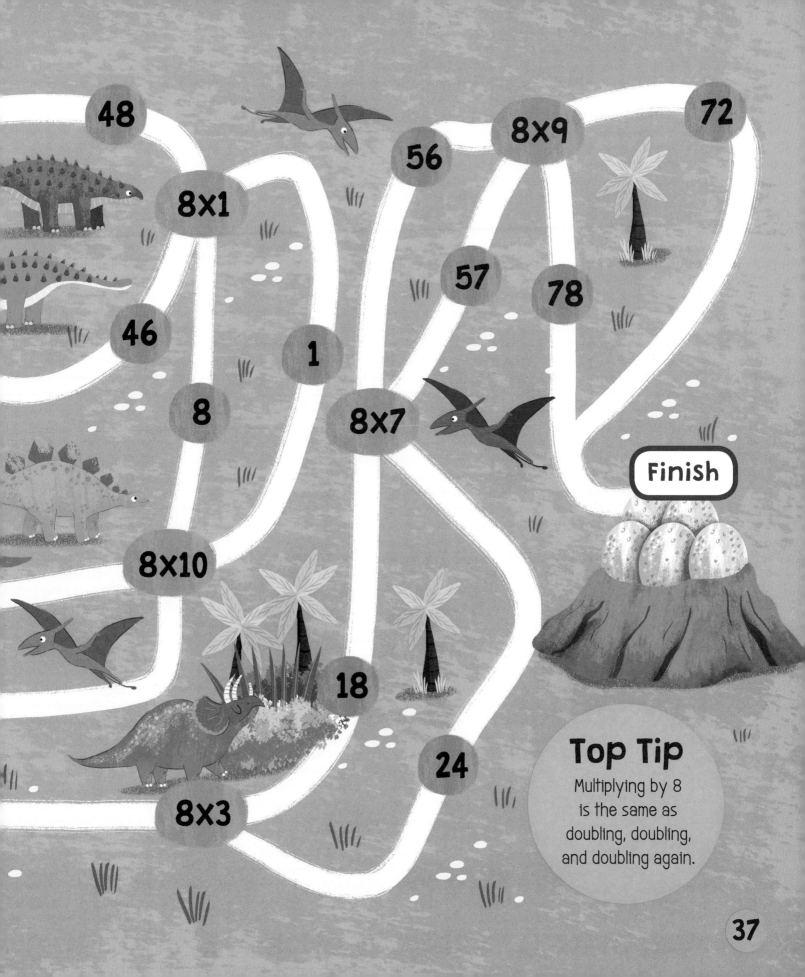

48

8x1

56

8x9

72

57

78

46

1

8

8x7

8x10

Finish

18

8x3

24

Top Tip
Multiplying by 8
is the same as
doubling, doubling,
and doubling again.

Divide by 8

Solve the problems and follow the route with the correct answers to lead the shoppers to the check out.

Start

$96 \div 8$

54

$48 \div 8$

11

$64 \div 8$

12

11

8

$80 \div 8$

10

Top Tip

Dividing by 8 can be tricky. Try halving, halving, and halving again.

38

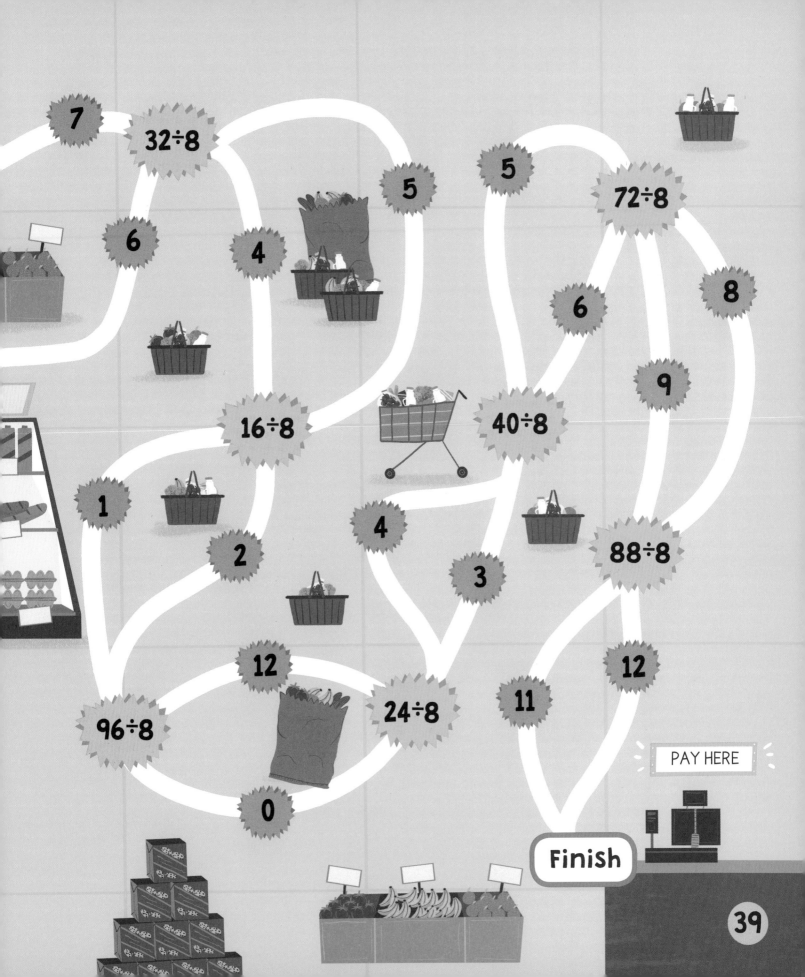

7

32÷8

6

5

5

72÷8

4

6

8

16÷8

40÷8

9

1

4

2

3

88÷8

12

11

12

96÷8

24÷8

0

PAY HERE

Finish

39

Mixed multiples 2, 4, and 8

Speed through the number problems and follow the correct answers to get the family to the airport in time!

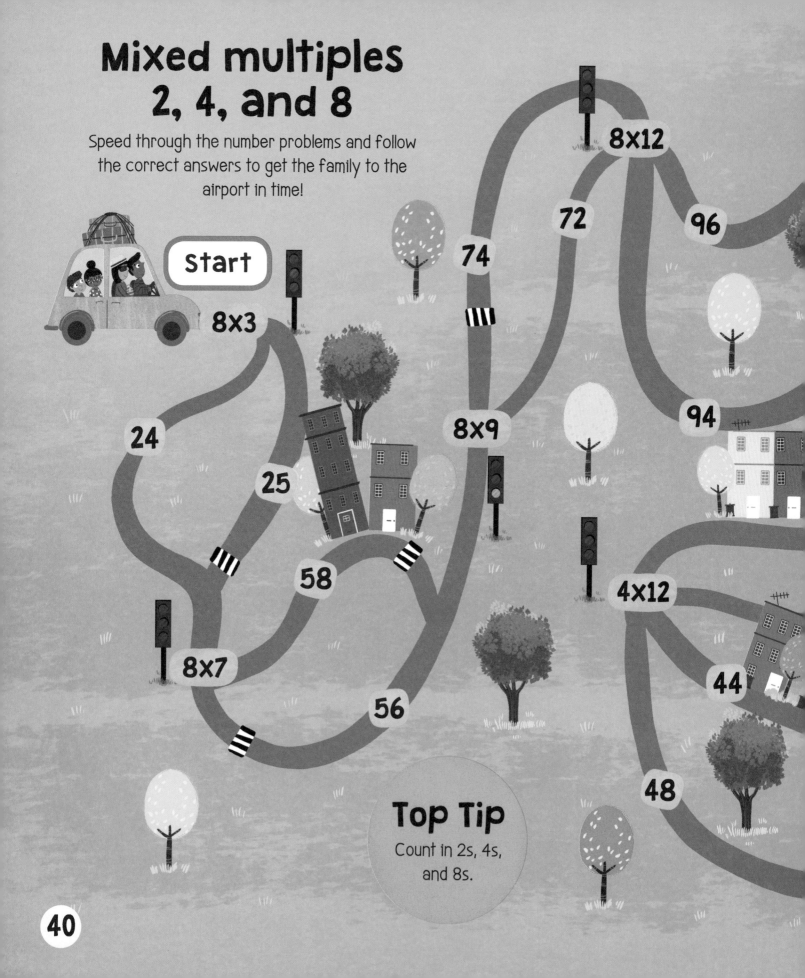

Start

8X3

8X12

72

96

74

8X9

94

24

25

58

4X12

8X7

44

56

48

Top Tip
Count in 2s, 4s, and 8s.

40

Mixed division 2, 4, and 8

Solve the problems and follow the path with the correct answers to lead the fox back to his den.

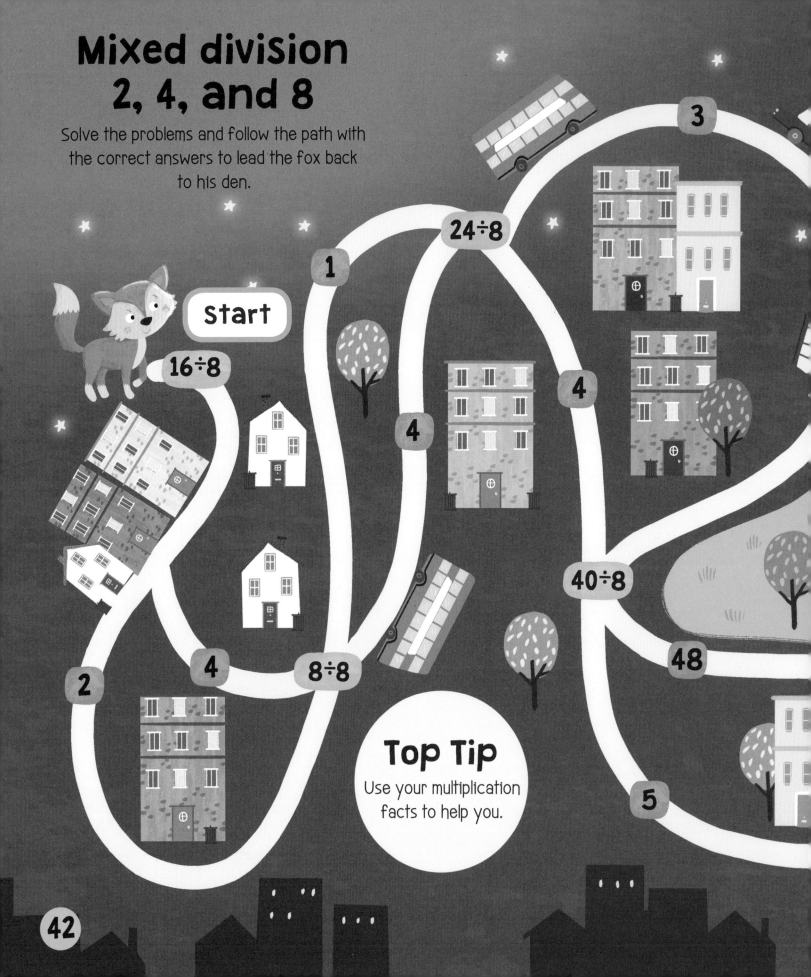

Start

16÷8

24÷8

1

3

4

4

40÷8

48

4

8÷8

2

4

5

Top Tip
Use your multiplication facts to help you.

43

Multiples of 3

Puff along the tracks following the numbers that are multiples of 3 to guide the steam train to the station.

24

38

12

37

3

7

9

28

27

18

Start

Top Tip

Try counting in 3s.

31

44

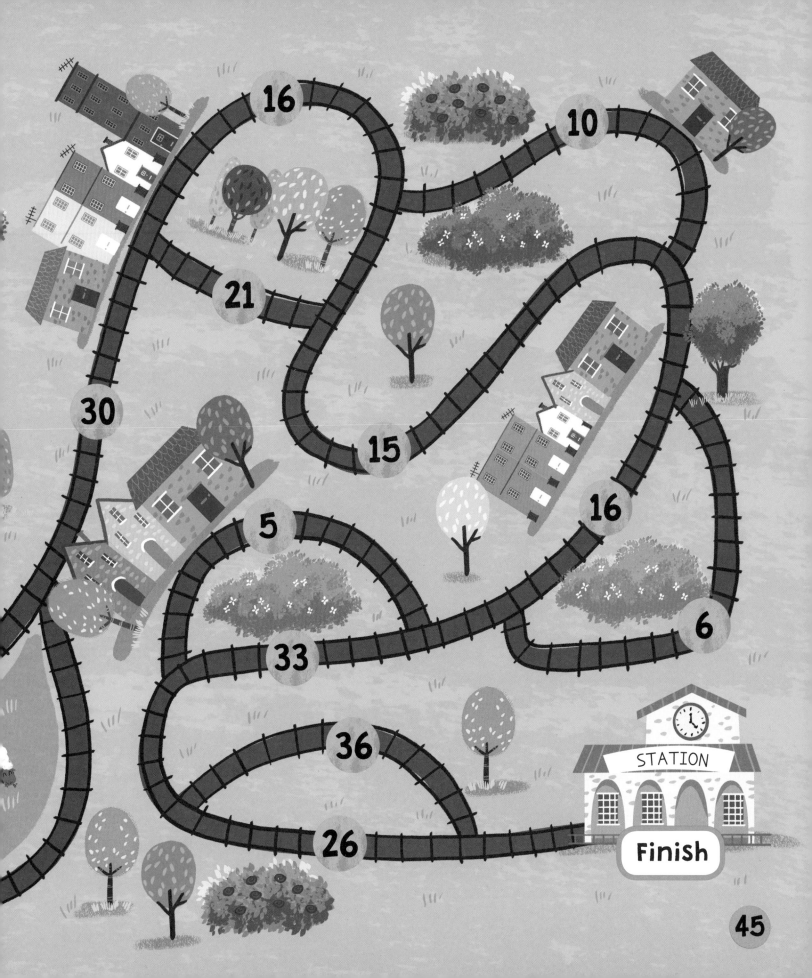

45

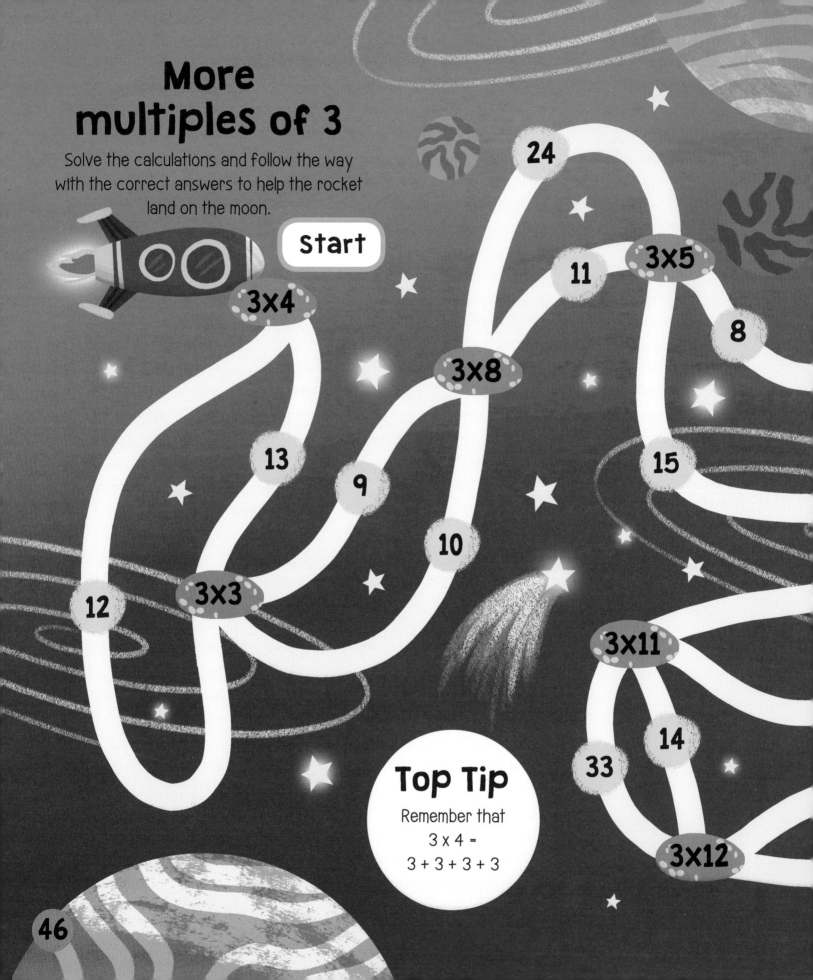

More multiples of 3

Solve the calculations and follow the way with the correct answers to help the rocket land on the moon.

Start

3x4

24

11   3x5

8

3x8

13

9   15

10

12   3x3

3x11

14

33

Top Tip

Remember that
3 x 4 =
3 + 3 + 3 + 3

3x12

46

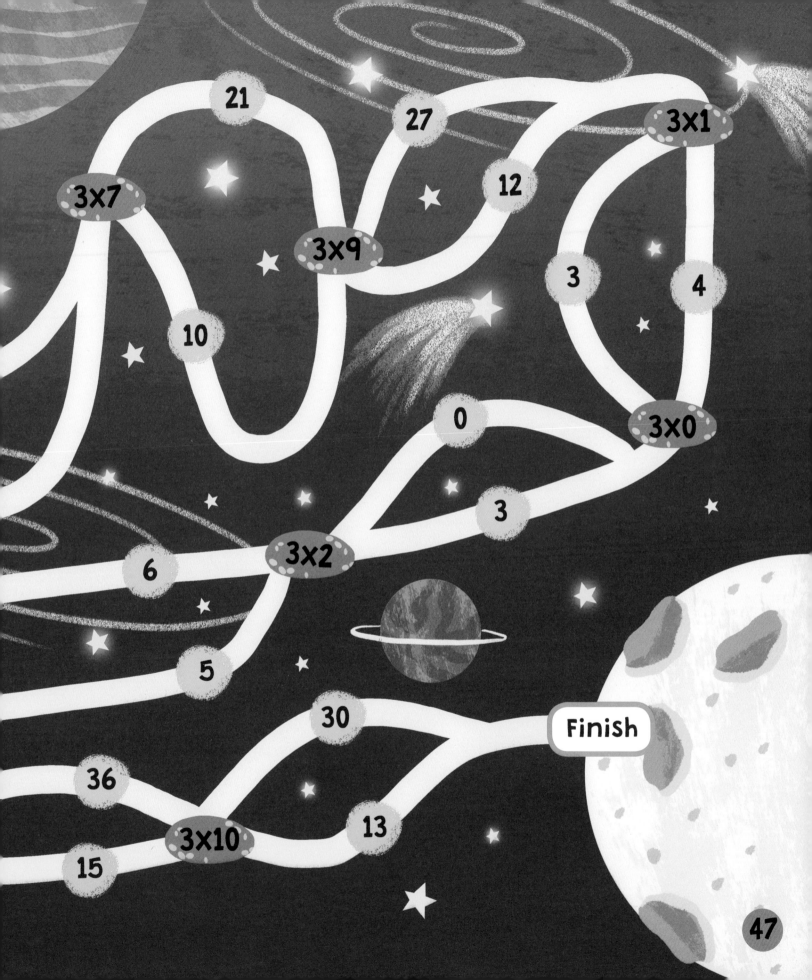

Divide by 3

Guide the children through the roads by following the route with the correct answers.

Start

18÷3

12

12

11

33÷3

36÷3

24

15

6

27÷3

9

30÷3

10

4

20

Top Tip

Share into three equal groups.

6÷3

5

2

3

6

24÷3

3

4

15÷3

7

12÷3

8

7

21÷3

9÷3

3

8

4

Finish

49

Multiples of 6

Ride the roller coaster back to the finish.
Follow the numbers that are multiples
of 6 to go the right way.

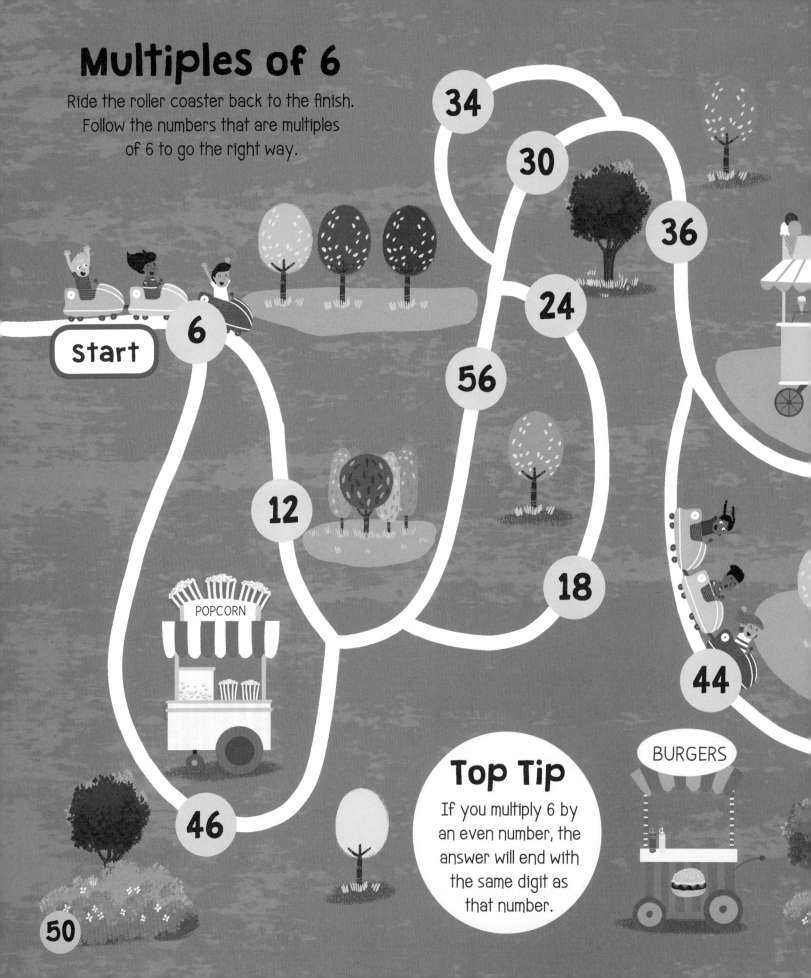

34

30

36

24

56

6

start

12

18

44

POPCORN

46

Top Tip

If you multiply 6 by
an even number, the
answer will end with
the same digit as
that number.

BURGERS

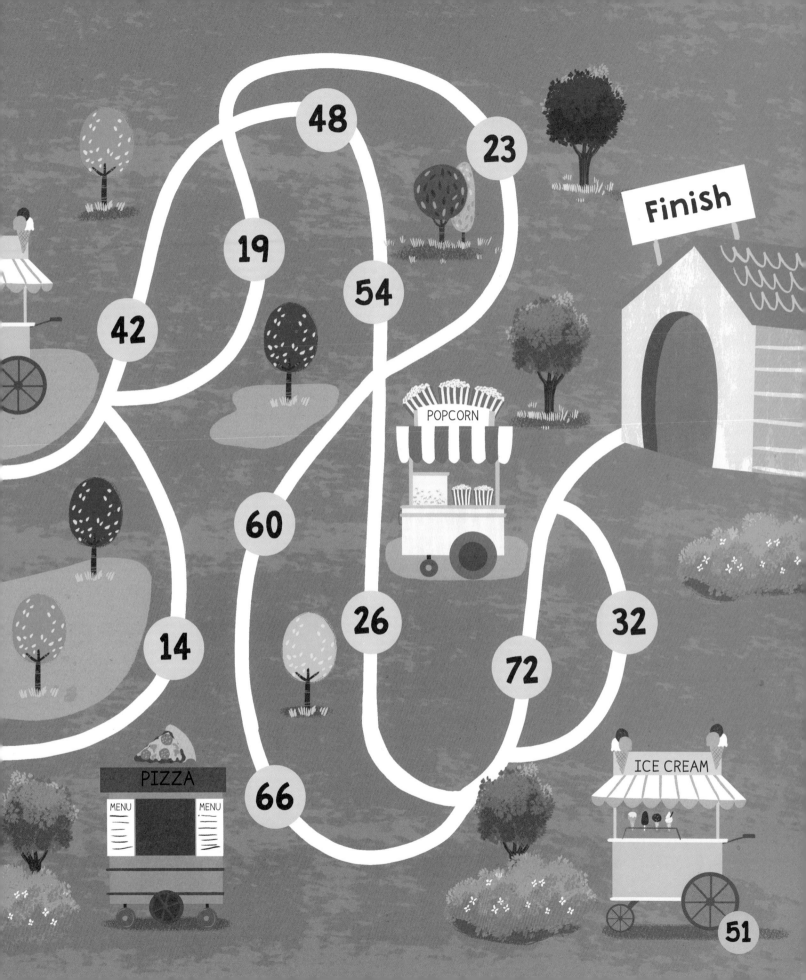

More multiples of 6

Help the boy find the bouncy castle at the funfair. Solve the multiplication problems and follow the path with the correct answers.

12

12

6×9

54

6×12

GHOST TR

6×2

18

8

9

72

66

6×3

Start

Top Tip

Remember that
6 x 4 =
6 + 6 + 6 + 6

Divide by 6

Help the police catch the burglars by solving the
calculations and following the correct answers.

9

60÷6   10

30÷6   5   24÷6   5

7   4   12

8   6   66÷6

11

42÷6

Start

54

36÷6

72÷6   10   12

6   7   1   6

54÷6

48÷6   7   6÷6   8   9

12÷6

3   2

8

Finish

55

Multiples of 9

Follow the numbers that are multiples of 9 to lead the scientist to the exit: it's time for a lunch break.

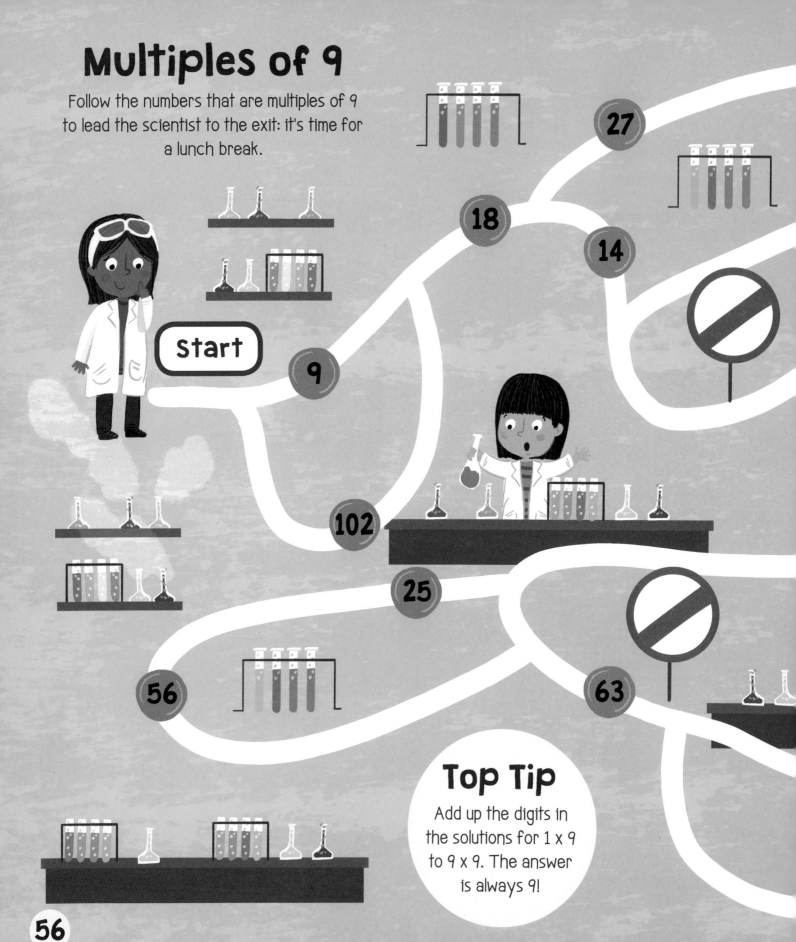

Start

27

18

14

9

102

25

56

63

Top Tip

Add up the digits in the solutions for 1 x 9 to 9 x 9. The answer is always 9!

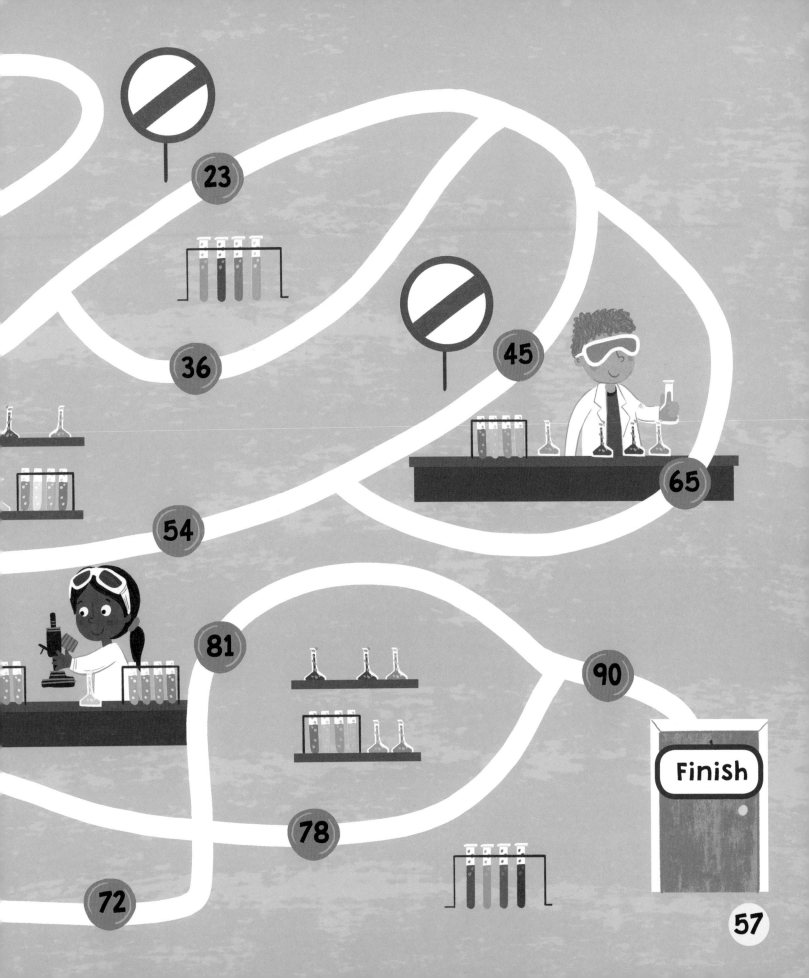

23

36

45

65

54

81

90

Finish

78

72

57

More multiples of 9

Solve the calculations and follow the correct answers to help the helicopter to safely reach the landing pad.

Start

9x12

9x9

80

81

90

109

108

9x11

99

89

9x10

91

Top Tip

Try counting in 9s:
$9 \times 2 = 9 + 9$

58

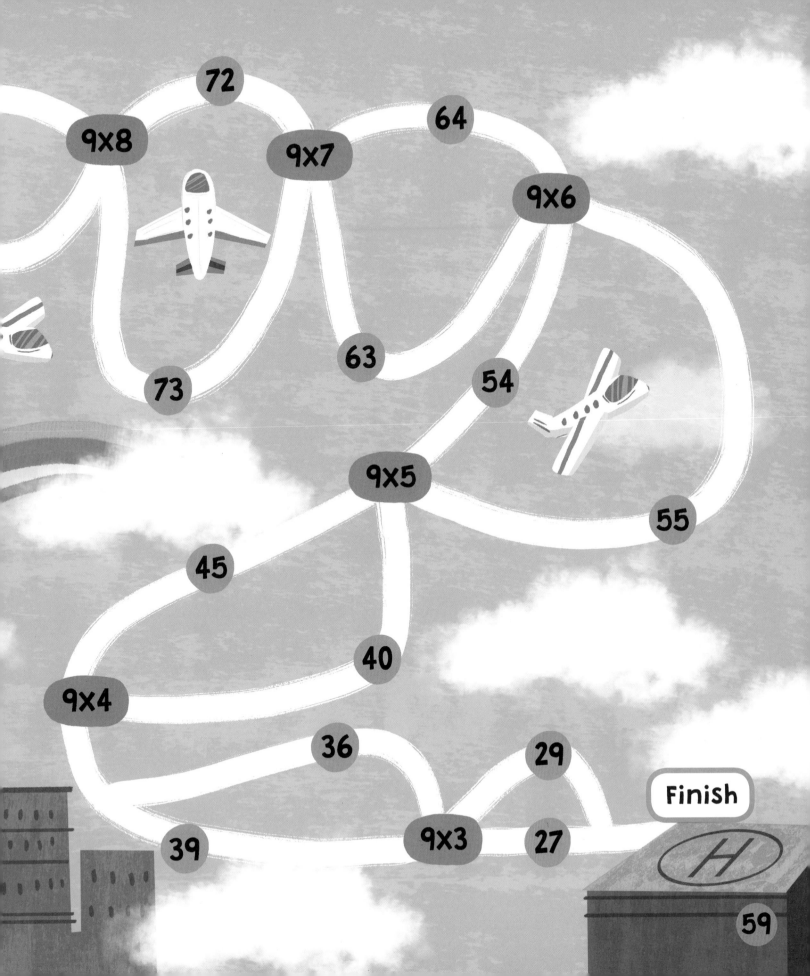

Divide by 9

Help the clown to find his juggling balls by solving the problems and following the correct answers.

ICE CREAM

11

81÷9

10

12

99÷9

90÷9

ICE CR

9

15

108÷9

63÷9

12

14

7

Start

60

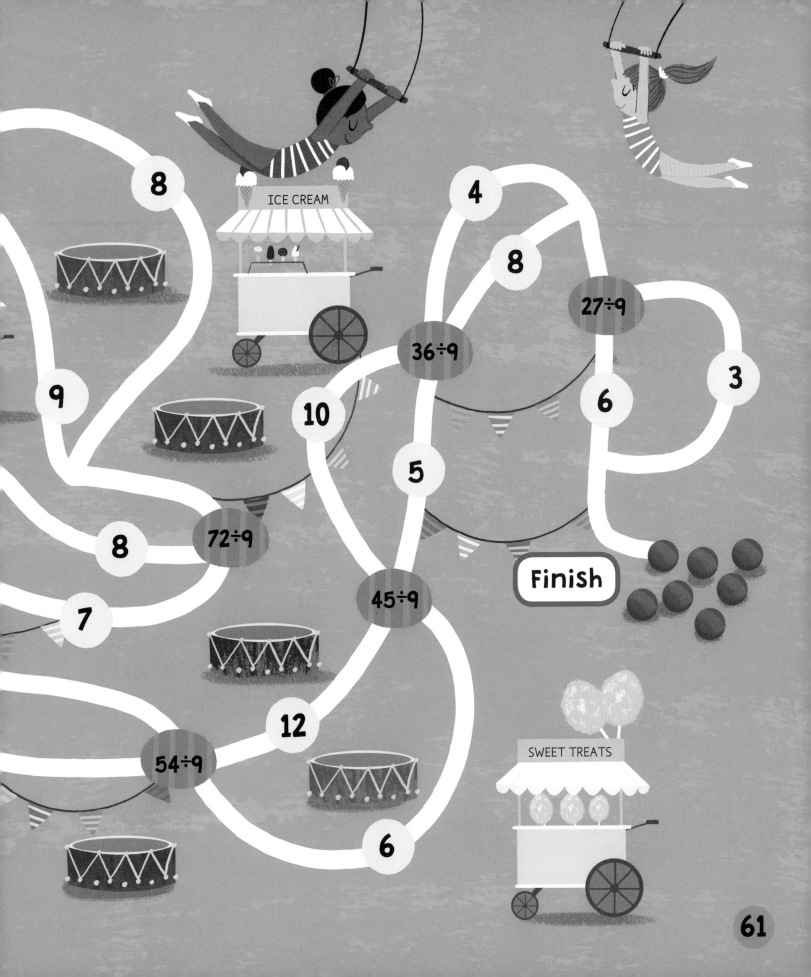

8

ICE CREAM

4

8

27÷9

36÷9

9

3

10

6

5

8

72÷9

Finish

7

45÷9

12

54÷9

SWEET TREATS

6

Mixed multiples of 3, 6, and 9

Help the pirate find the treasure.
Solve the calculations and follow the
correct answers.

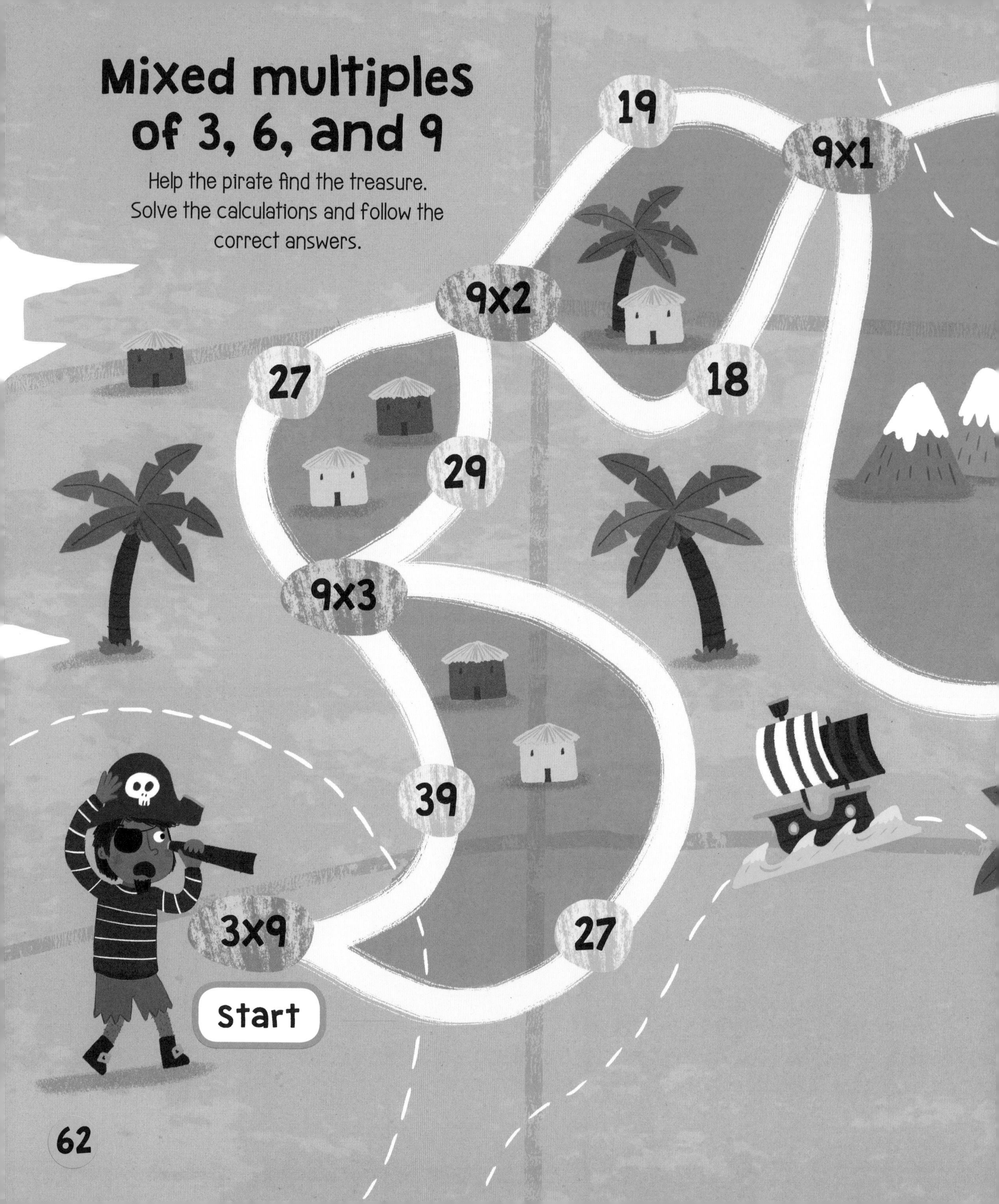

19

9×1

9×2

27

18

29

9×3

39

3×9

27

Start

62

63

Divide and multiply 3, 6, and 9

The delivery van needs help delivering the parcels. Solve the calculations and follow the correct answers to guide the truck to the house with the green door.

5

$36 \div 9$

6

$45 \div 9$

6

7

4

3

$54 \div 9$

$66 \div 6$

8

7

$63 \div 9$

Start

64

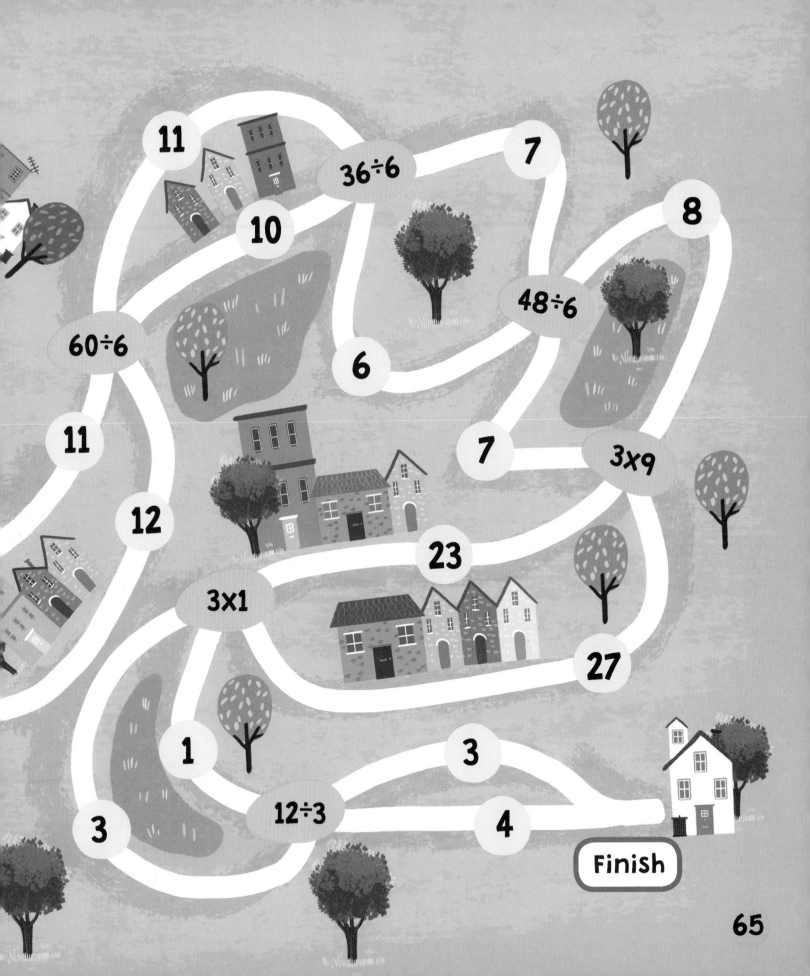

11   36÷6   7

10

8

60÷6   48÷6

6

11

7   3×9

12

23

3×1

27

1   3

3

12÷3   4   Finish

65

Multiples of 11

Follow the numbers that are multiples of 11 to lead the baby dragon back to his mother.

Start

66

61

55

11

34

31

99

33

111

88

21

77

120

Top Tip

To multiply a single-digit number by 11, just write the same number again, next to it!

Divide by 11

Guide the mermaid to the pearl by solving the calculations and following the correct answers.

3

4

66÷11

8

11

77÷11

33÷11

6

7

14

44÷11

4

Start

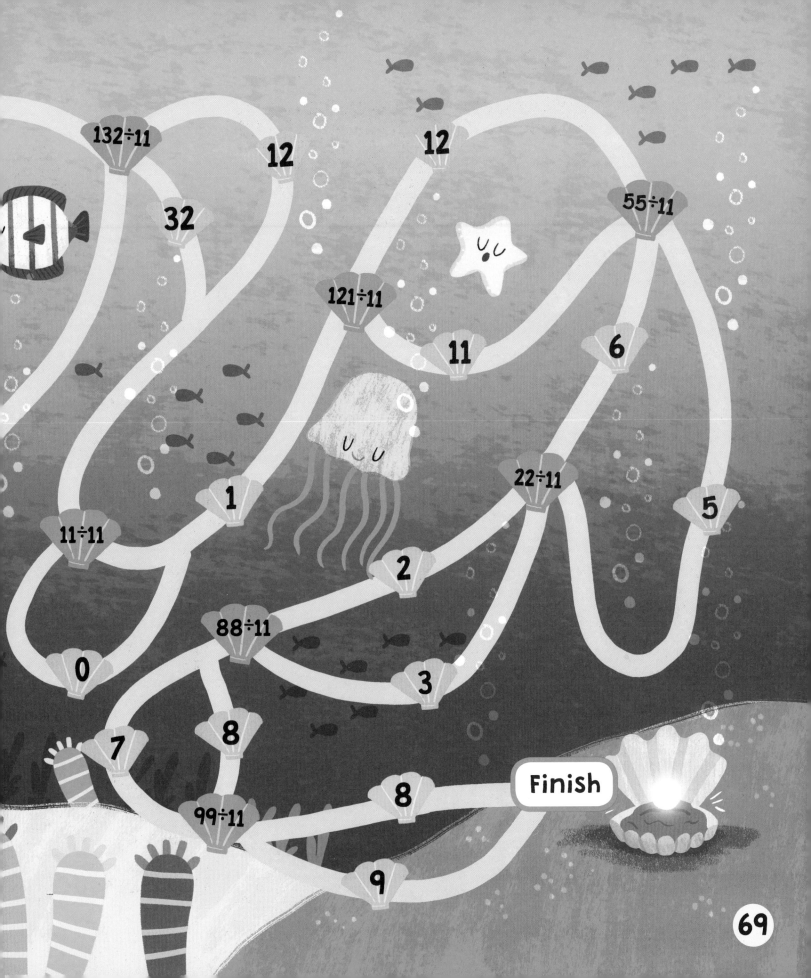

132÷11   12   12   55÷11

32

121÷11   11   6

11÷11   1   22÷11   5

0   2

88÷11   3

8

7

99÷11   8   Finish

9

69

Multiples of 12

Follow the numbers that are multiples of 12 to help the children row back to the campsite.

Start

12

22

24

66

60

78

72

88

38

36

48

84

46

70

Top Tip

If you know your 2 times table and your 10 times table, add together the solutions.

96

110

108

120

140

130

132

44

144

8

Finish

Divide by 12

Guide the children to the other end of the campsite. Solve the problems and follow the path with the correct answers.

9

108÷12

20

120÷12

8

13

11

8

10

132÷12

72÷12

5

12

6

14

144÷12

Top Tip
Remember that division is the opposite of multiplication.

Start

72

Mixed 10, 11, 12 multiplication

Speed to the finish line by solving the multiplication questions and follow the path with the correct answers.

Start

10x2

50

15

11x6

10x5

20

12

66

22

24

60

11x2

12x2

21

Top Tip
Watch out: it's mixed multiplication!

22

74

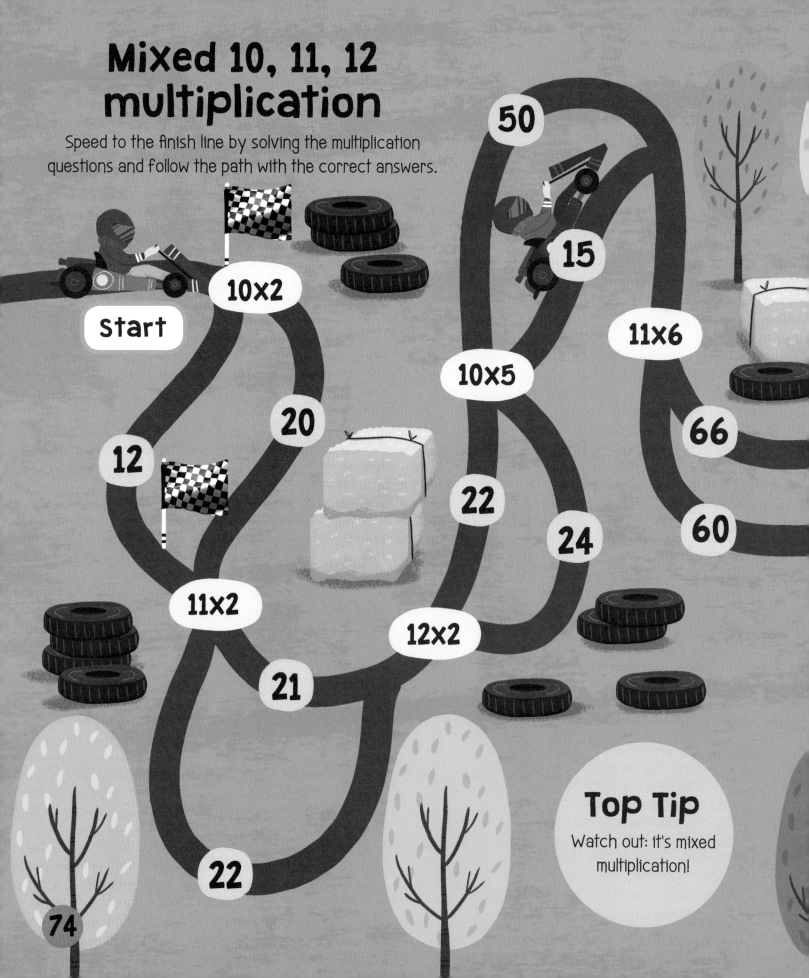

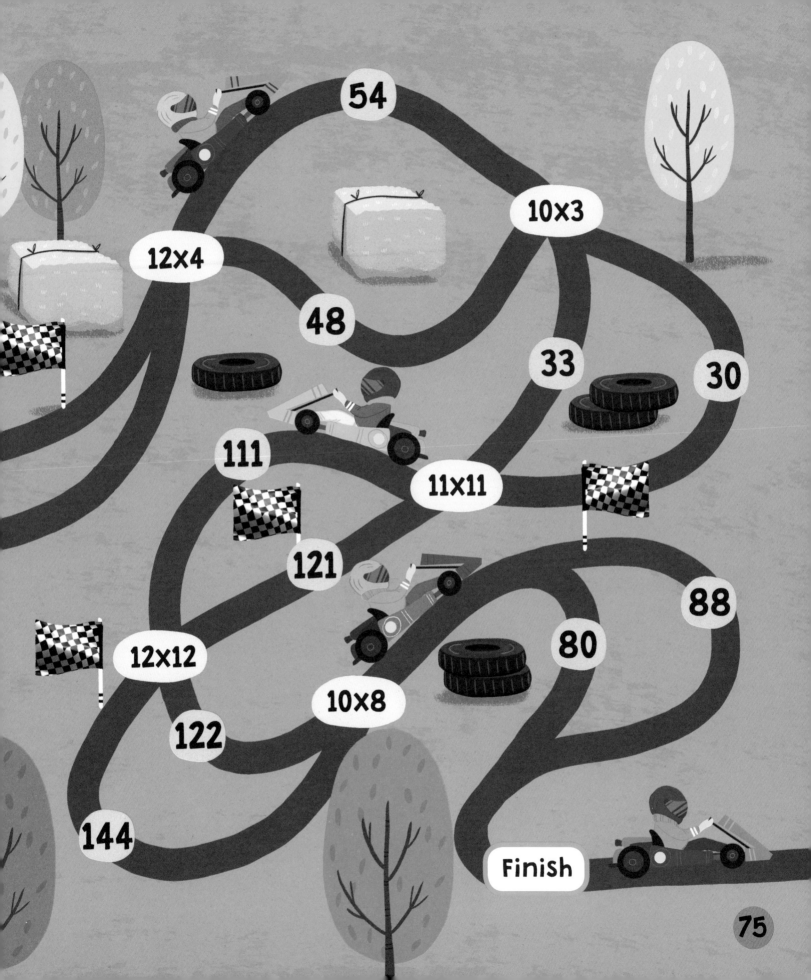

54

10×3

12×4

48

33

30

111

11×11

121

88

12×12

80

10×8

122

144

Finish

75

Mixed multiply and divide by 2

Solve the calculations and follow the path with the correct answers to get to the finish line.

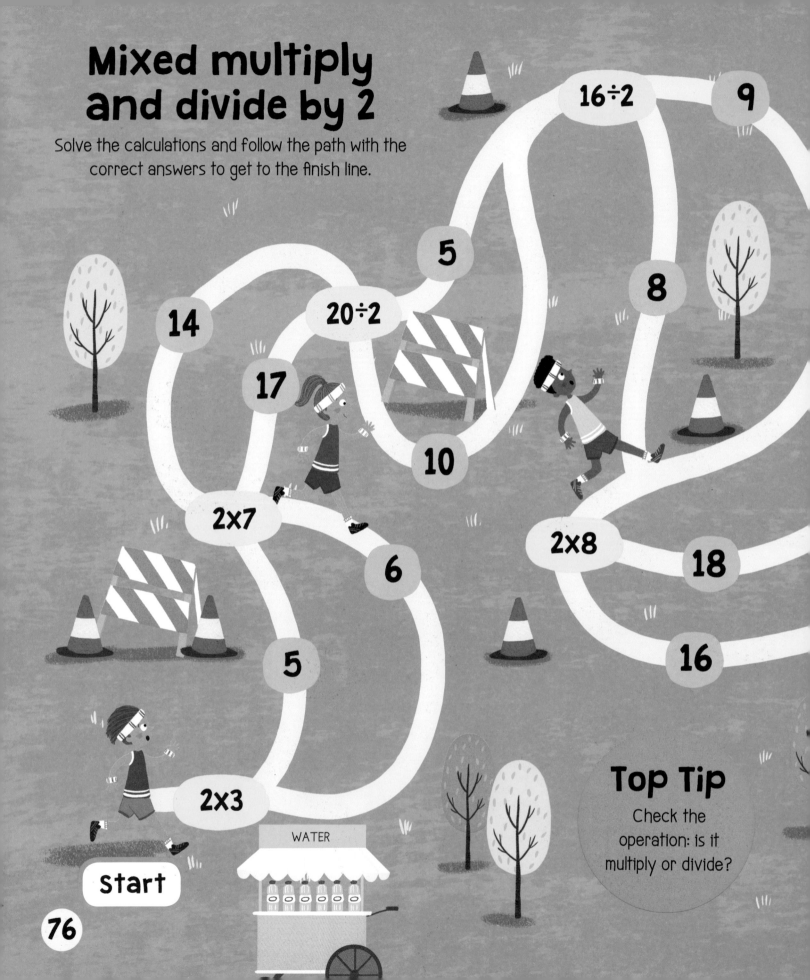

16÷2

9

5

14

20÷2

8

17

10

2x7

2x8

18

6

5

16

2x3

WATER

Start

76

Top Tip

Check the operation: is it multiply or divide?

Mixed multiply and divide by 5

Help the boy find his way through the cave by solving the problems, following the route with the correct answers.

Start

25÷5

5x7

37

4

5

5

20

20÷5

5x3

8

15

Top Tip

Multiplying 5 by an odd number gives you an answer ending with 5. Multiplying 5 by an even number give you an answer ending with 0.

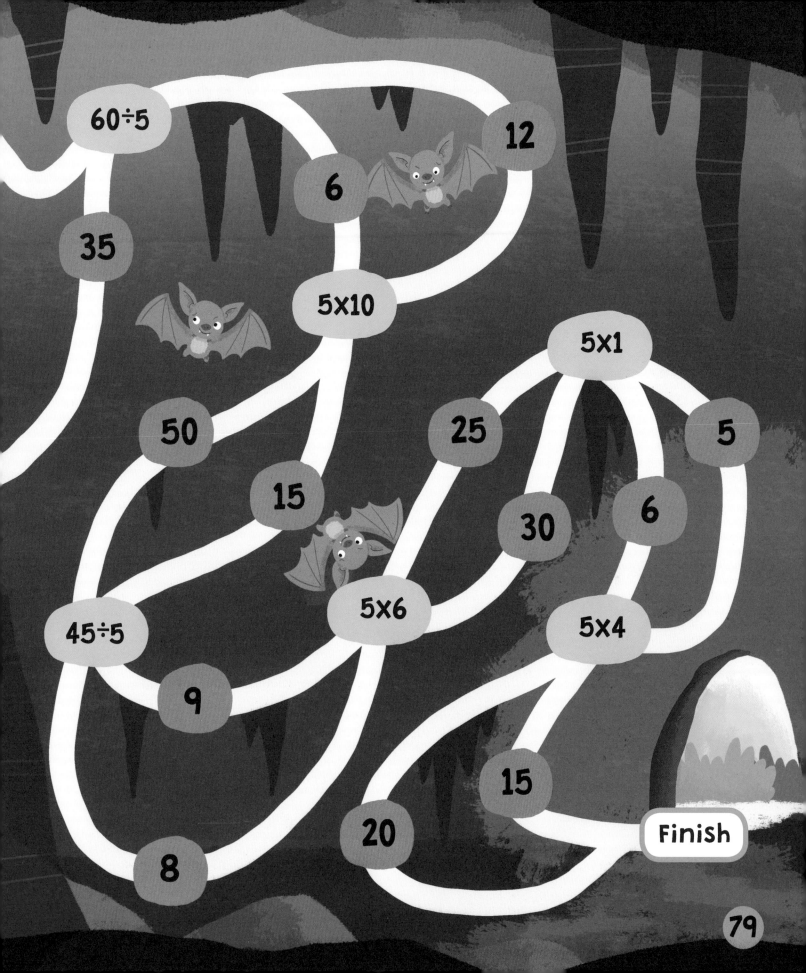

60÷5

12

6

35

5x10

5x1

50

25

5

15

6

30

45÷5

5x6

5x4

9

15

8

20

Finish

Multiples of 100

The girl has dropped her fishing net: follow the numbers that are multiples of 100 to help her find it.

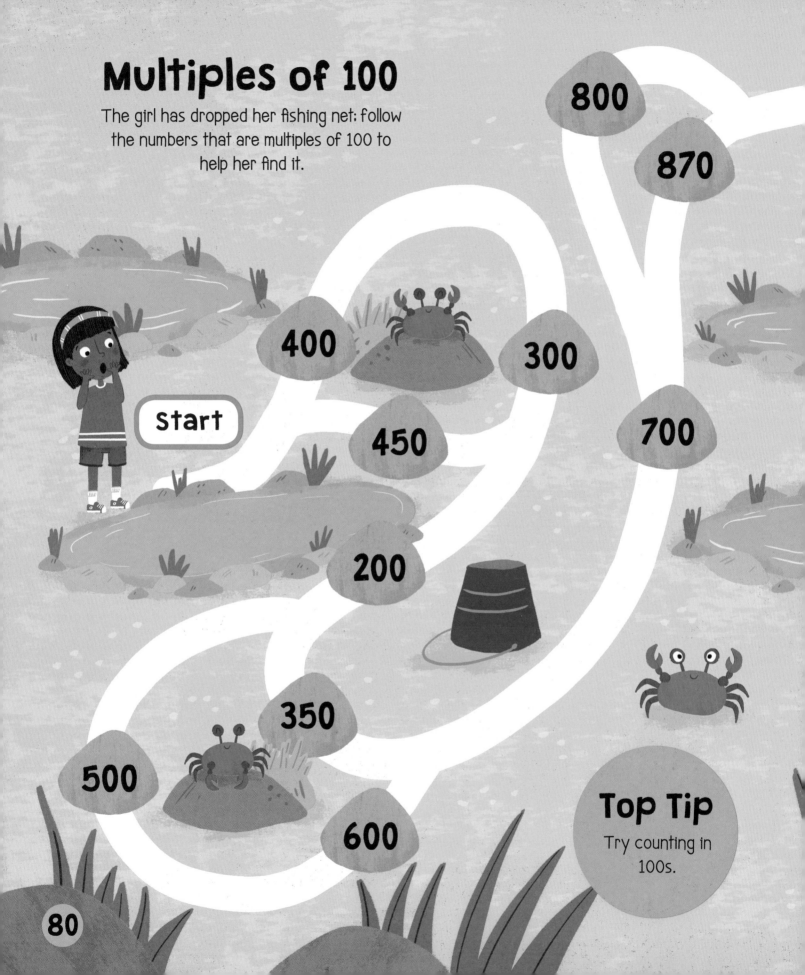

Start

800

870

400

300

450

700

200

350

500

600

Top Tip
Try counting in 100s.

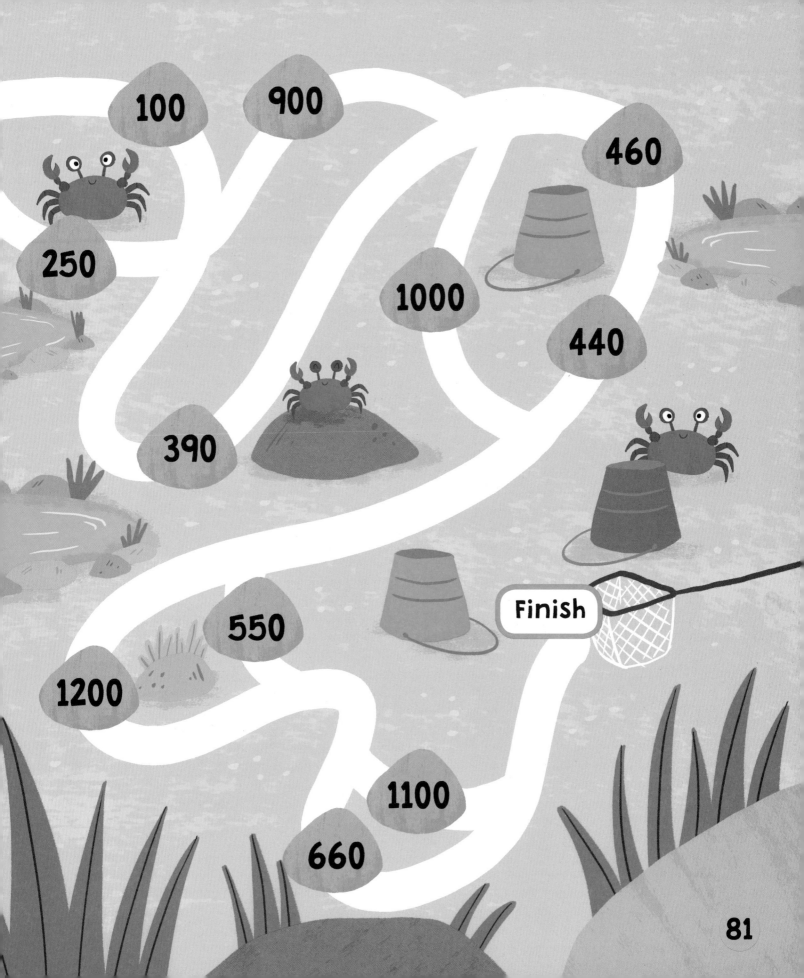

100

900

460

250

1000

440

390

550

1200

Finish

1100

660

Divide by 100

Guide the fairy through the magical forest and back to the fairy door. Solve the calculations and follow the correct answers.

Start

$200 \div 100$

20

2

$300 \div 100$

$500 \div 100$

50

9

$900 \div 100$

90

30

3

Top Tip

Remember division is the opposite of multiplication:
$200 \div 100 = ?$
$? \times 100 = 200$

82

Multiples of 50

Follow the numbers that are multiples of 50 to help the fly escape the spiders' web.

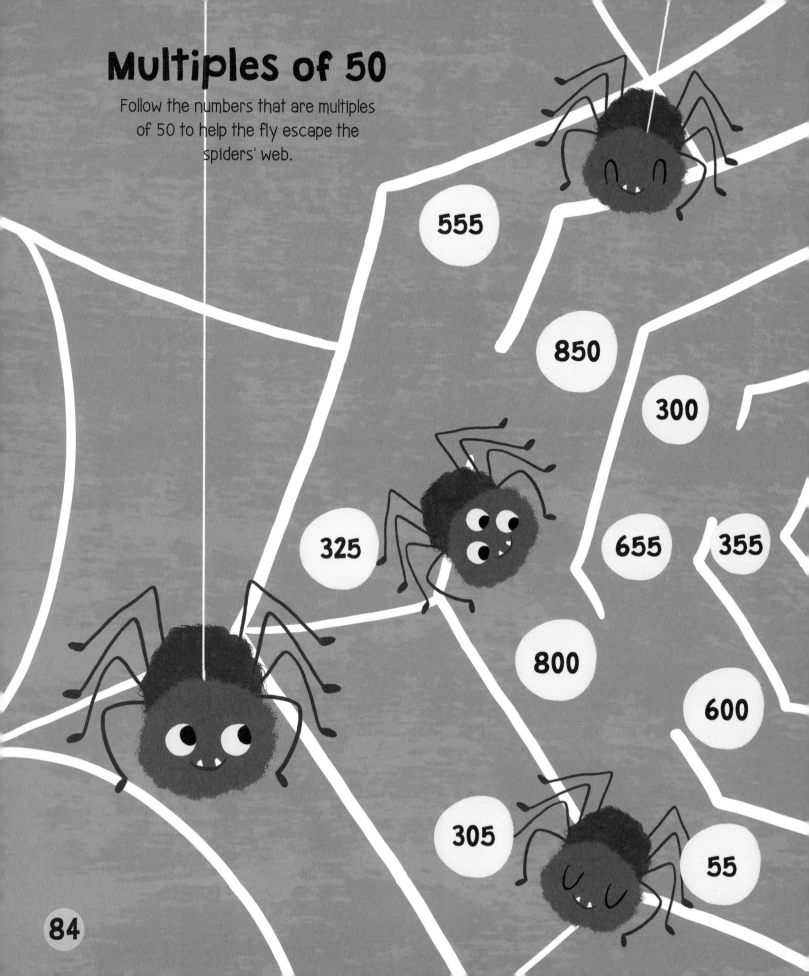

555

850

300

325

655

355

800

600

305

55

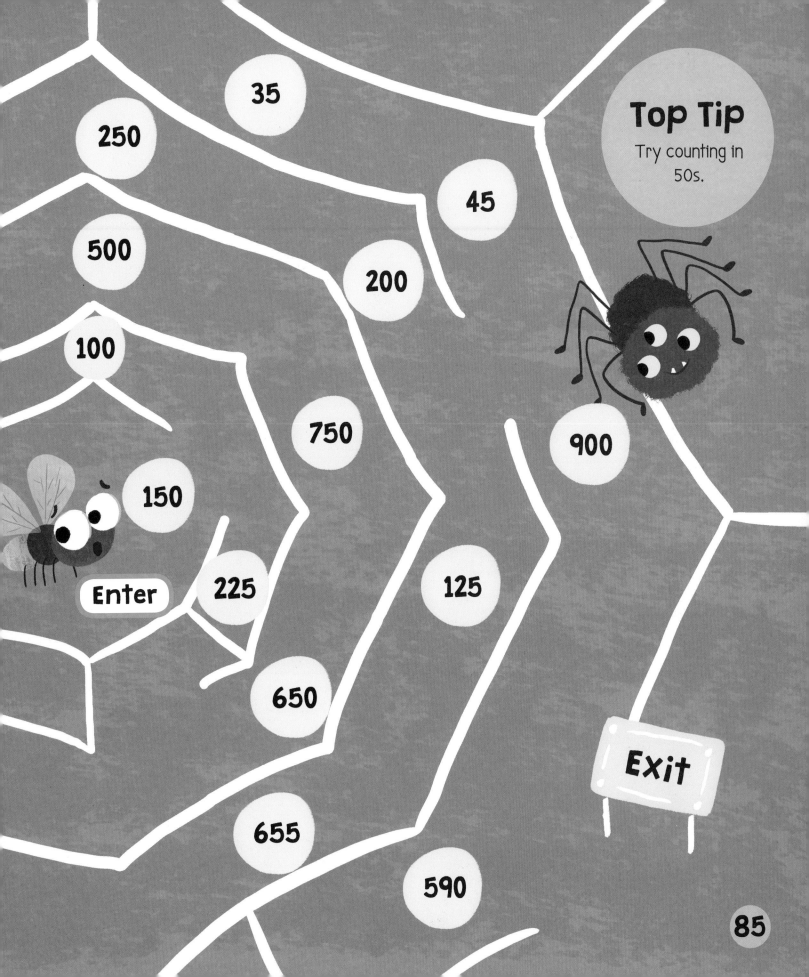

Divide by 50

Help the girl get to school as quickly as possible, but watch out for the puddles. Solve the calculations and follow the correct answers.

$100 \div 50$

10

5

12

1

2

$50 \div 50$

$600 \div 50$

$200 \div 50$

20

3

$250 \div 50$

13

3

$150 \div 50$

4

Start

Top Tip

Remember division is the opposite of multiplication:
$300 \div 50 = ?$
$? \times 50 = 300$

5

350÷50

8

7

4

400÷50

300÷50

5

4

8

6

100

500÷50

10

110

550÷50

11

Finish

SCHOOL

87

Multiples of 25

Follow the numbers that are multiples of 25 to guide the safari truck back to the lodge.

55

Start

25

355

75

100

50

255

65

LODGE

125

135

155

175

Finish

Top Tip

Try counting in 25s.

150

ANSWERS

4-5 Doubles

6-7 Multiples of 2

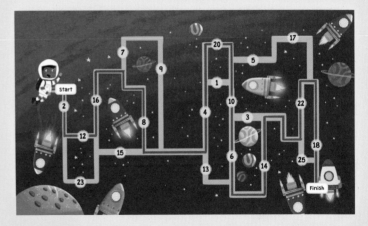

8-9 More multiples of 2

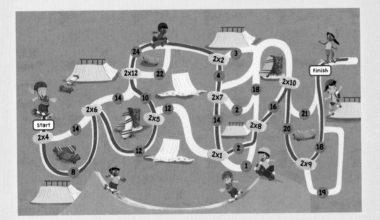

10-11 Divide by 2

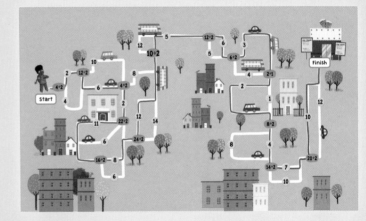

12–13 Multiples of 10

14–15 More multiples of 10

16–17 Divide by 10

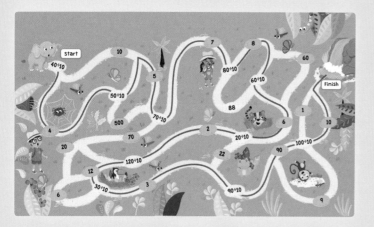

18–19 Multiples of 5

20–21 More multiples of 5

22–23 Divide by 5

24-25 Mixed multiples 2, 5, and 10.

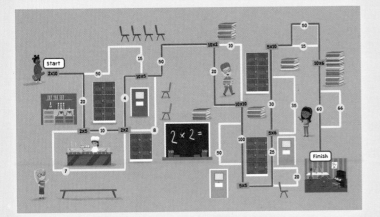

26-27 Mixed division 2, 5, and 10

28-29 Multiples of 4

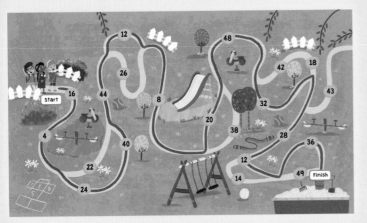

30-31 More multiples of 4

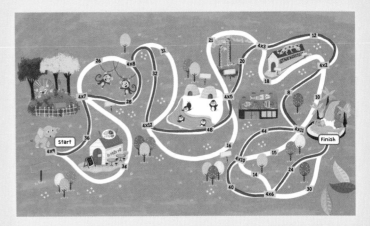

32-33 Divide by 4

34-35 Multiples of 8

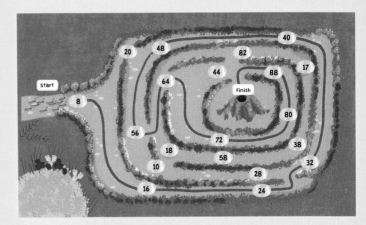

36–37 More multiples of 8

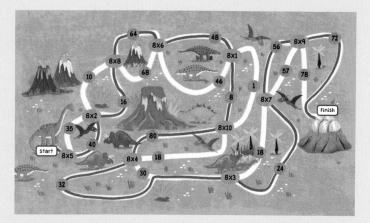

38–39 Divide by 8

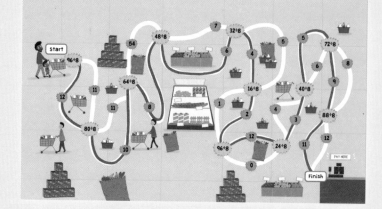

40–41 Mixed multiples 2, 4, and 8

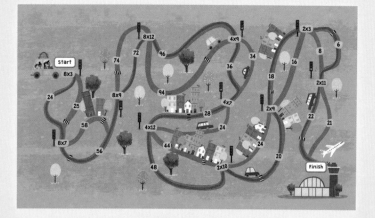

42–43 Mixed division 2, 4, and 8

44–45 Multiples of 3

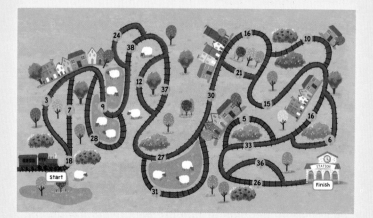

46–47 More multiples of 3

48–49 Divide by 3

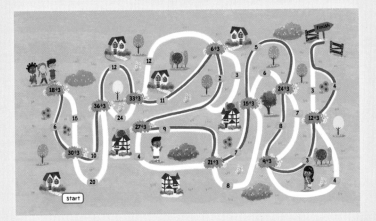

50–51 Multiples of 6

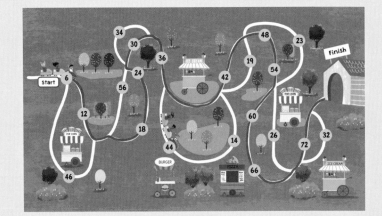

52–53 More multiples of 6

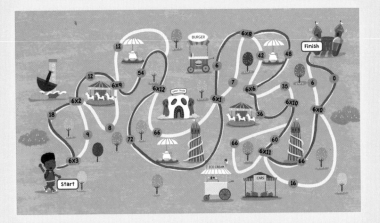

54–55 Divide by 6

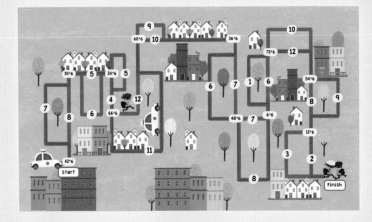

56–57 Multiples of 9

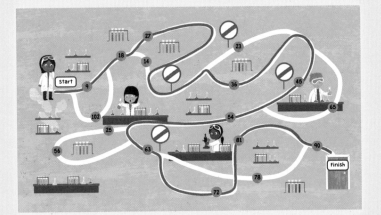

58–59 More multiples of 9

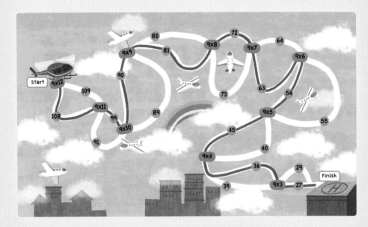

60–61 Divide by 9

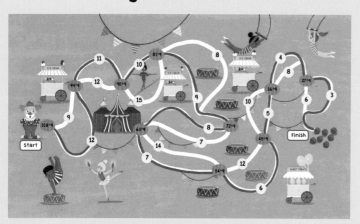

62–63 Mixed multiples of 3, 6, and 9

64–65 Divide and multiply 3, 6, and 9

66–67 Multiples of 11

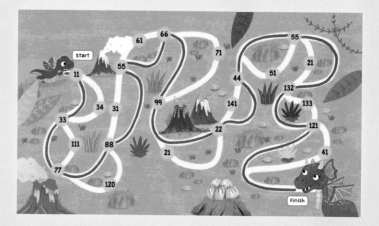

68–69 Divide by 11

70–71 Multiples of 12

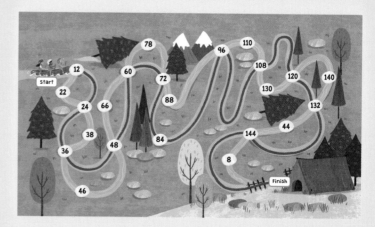

72-73 Divide by 12

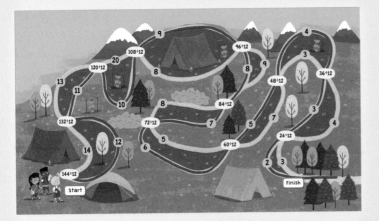

74-75 Mixed 10, 11, 12 multiplication

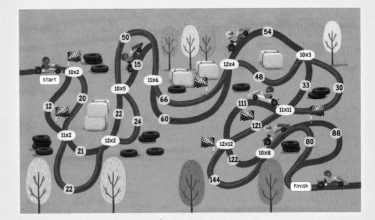

76-77 Mixed multiply and divide by 2

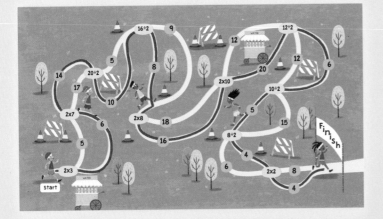

78-79 Mixed multiply and divide by 5

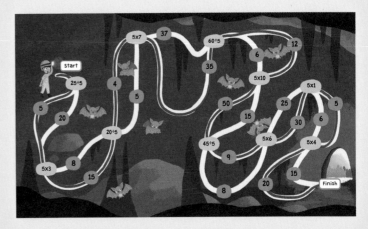

80-81 Multiples of 100

82-83 Divide by 100

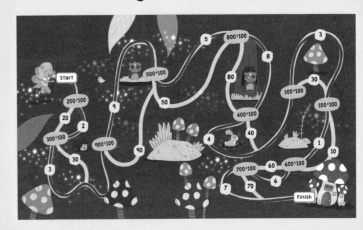

84–85 Multiples of 50

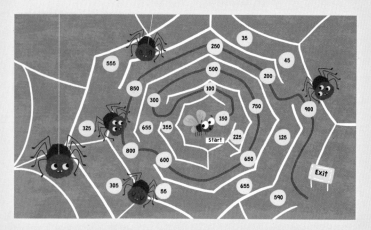

86–87 Divide by 50

88 Multiples of 25